WEIRD WEATHER

TEMPERATURE EXTREMES

JOANNE MATTERN

Enslow PUBLISHING

I0876239

Please visit our website, www.enslow.com. For a free color catalog of all our high-quality books,
call toll free 1-800-398-2504 or fax 1-877-980-4454

Copyright © 2027 by Enslow Publishing

Published in 2027 by
Enslow Publishing
2544 Clinton Street
Buffalo, NY 14224

All rights reserved.

No part of this book may be reproduced by any means without the written permission of the publisher.

Cataloging-in-Publication Data
Names: Mattern, Joanne, 1963-.
Title: Temperature extremes / Joanne Mattern.
Description: Buffalo, NY : Enslow Publishing, 2027. | Series: Weird weather | Includes glossary.
Identifiers: ISBN 9781978549814 (pbk.) | ISBN 9781978549821 (library bound) | ISBN 9781978549838 (ebook)
Subjects: LCSH: Temperature--Juvenile literature. | Heat--Juvenile literature. | Cold--Juvenile literature. | Weather--Juvenile literature.
Classification: LCC QC271.4 M375 2027 | DDC 536.5--dc23

Photos Credits: Cover, p.1 ©2013 Seqoya/Shutterstock.com; p.3 and throughout the book ©2020 Cherisha Kay Norman/Shutterstock.com; p.4 ©2015 Greta Gabaglio/Shutterstock.com; p.5 ©2014 Jason Patrick Ross/Shutterstock.com; p.6 ©2020 Tomas Ragina/Shutterstock.com; p.6, p.7, p.14, p.28 ©2024 Marina Poushkina/Shutterstock.com; p.8 ©2017 baseart/Shutterstock.com; p.9 ©2006 Natalia Bratslavsky/Shutterstock.com; p.10 ©2024 Vladimir Potapeknko/Shutterstock.com; p.10 CC4 Arctic and Antarctic Research Institute https://creativecommons.org/licenses/by/4.0/; p.11 ©2018 Sergey 402/Shutterstock.com; p.12, p.13, p.14 ©2016 Wojciech Dziadosz/Shutterstock.com; p.15 ©2019 Aitor Gonzalez Frias/Shutterstock.com; p.16, p.17, p.29 ©2019 Iryna Marienko/Shutterstock.com; p.18 ©2020 Ben Wickham/Shutterstock.com; p.18 ©2025 Piyaset/Shutterstock.com; p.19 ©2023 Scott Harvey Aerials/Shutterstock.com; p.19 ©2018 Urban Images/Shutterstock.com; p.20, p.29 ©2019 Daniel Toh/Shutterstock.com; p.21 ©2022 Lukas Ruetz/Shutterstock.com; p.22, p.23 ©2016 Irit/Shutterstock.com; p.24, p.25, p.29 ©2017 Tom Wang/Shutterstock.com; p.26 ©2022 Marc Bruxelle/Shutterstock.com; p.27, p.28 ©2017 tome213/Shutterstock.com

Printed in China

CPSIA compliance information: Batch #QSENS27: For further information, contact Enslow Publishing, New York, New York, at 1-800-398-2504.

Find us on

TABLE OF CONTENTS

Words in the glossary appear in **bold** type the first time they are used in the text.

Is It Hot in Here?

Does it get very hot where you live? Many places on Earth can get very warm. But some places go to temperature extremes!

The hottest temperature ever recorded was at Furnace Creek Ranch in Death Valley, California. On July 10, 1913, the thermometer went to a whopping 134.1 degrees Fahrenheit (56.7 degrees Celsius)! If you went outside that day, it would feel like walking into an oven. You could only stay outside for a few minutes. You would immediately start to sweat. Your body would lose too much water. Staying outside in super-high temperatures can kill you!

Death Valley is a very hot place. Temperatures rise higher than 120 degrees Fahrenheit (49 degrees Celsius) all the time. But other places on Earth are very hot too. A temperature of 129.2 degrees Fahrenheit (54 degrees Celsius) was recorded in Kuwait in 2016.

For years, scientists thought the hottest temperature ever recorded was 136.4 degrees Fahrenheit (58 degrees Celsius). That was in Libya in 1922. Later, scientists decided this measurement was not **accurate**. The thermometer was not working correctly. The wrong information might have been recorded. Even so, it was still a very hot day!

HOW HOT WAS IT?

*Some scientists also doubt the 1913 record is true. They point out that **instruments** used to measure temperatures back then were not as accurate as the ones used today.*

WHY SO HOT?

The hot places in California, Kuwait, and Libya all have one thing in common. They are all deserts.

Deserts are the kings of temperature extremes. That's because they have little water and few clouds. The sun heats up the ground during the day. At night, there are no clouds to stop that heat from rising back up into the air. So, days are very hot. Nights are very cold.

HOLD IN THE HEAT

Death Valley is below sea level. But it is surrounded by mountains. Those mountains trap hot air down in the valley.

C-C-C-COLD!

It's so cold, your teeth are chattering! Just be glad you weren't at the Vostok Research Center in Antarctica on July 21, 1983. That's when the temperature plunged to –128.6 degrees Fahrenheit (–89 degrees Celsius). Most of the coldest air temperatures on Earth are at the Vostok Station.

But wait! Sometimes the ground is even colder than the air. Scientists on the East Antarctic **Plateau** measured snow **surface** temperatures as low as –144 degrees Fahrenheit (–98 degrees Celsius). Brrr!

AN ICY LOCATION

The Vostok Research Center sits on 2.3 miles (3.7 kilometers) of ice. No wonder it's so cold!

Antarctica is the coldest place on Earth. But did you know Antarctica is actually a desert? You might picture a desert covered with sand. But a desert is a place that is very dry. The inner part of Antarctica receives less than two inches (five centimeters) of **precipitation** a year.

If it hardly snows in Antarctica, why is it covered with snow and ice? The snow and ice in Antarctica have been there for thousands of years! It is too cold to melt much.

COLD REFLECTIONS

The snow and ice on Antarctica's surface reflect sunlight instead of holding it. This is another reason the continent is so cold.

ON THE FRONT LINES

Death Valley is hot most of the time. Antarctica is cold all of the time. But most places can go from hot to cold and back again. These wild weather changes are caused by fronts.

A cold front happens when a mass of cold air overtakes an area of warmer air. A warm front happens when a mass of warm air overtakes cooler air. When these masses move over an area, the temperature can change. Sometimes, this change is **gradual**. Other times, it happens very quickly.

Cold fronts can make wild changes in the weather. On February 20, 2018, a cold front dropped temperatures in Oklahoma City, Oklahoma, more than 21 degrees Fahrenheit (12 degrees Celsius) in just four minutes! Temperatures plunged from 64.4 degrees Fahrenheit (18 degrees Celsius) to 43 degrees Fahrenheit (six degrees Celsius) that morning.

But that's not even the most extreme temperature drop. On November 9, 1911, a blast of cold air hit Rapid City, South Dakota. It was 55 degrees Fahrenheit (12.7 degrees Celsius) at six o'clock in the morning. By eight o'clock, the temperature was a chilly three degrees Fahrenheit (–16 degrees Celsius)!

TWISTERS!

The weather front that hit Rapid City also caused several dangerous tornadoes.

WILD WARMUPS

What about when the temperature rises quickly? This seems to happen a lot in Montana. Scientists have recorded many temperature swings there.

The most extreme warmup happened in mid-January 1972. Temperatures in Loma, Montana, went from –54 degrees Fahrenheit (–48 degrees Celsius) on the morning of January 14, to 49 degrees Fahrenheit (9.4 degrees Celsius) 24 hours later. That's a difference of 103 degrees Fahrenheit (57.2 degrees Celsius)!

LOMA, MONTANA

WINDS AND BURSTS

Some extreme warmups are caused by Chinook winds. Chinook winds are warm, dry winds that flow down a mountain when the air on top has lost its **moisture**. These winds often happen in the Rocky Mountains. Warm air from the Pacific Ocean drops its moisture over the mountains. It leaves warm, dry air to blow down the other side.

These winds also happen in other parts of the world. In Europe, they are called föhn winds. In central Asia, they are called afghanet winds. South Americans call these winds Puelche.

WHAT'S IN A NAME?

The word Chinook *means "snow eater." It is also the name of an Indigenous American tribe in Oregon.*

Heat bursts are rare events that can send temperatures shooting way up. These bursts usually happen when thunderstorms are about to end. When rain falls into a layer of very dry air below the cloud, it evaporates and cools the air around it. The dense air falls quickly toward Earth and warms up. This action creates a blast of heat. Temperatures can rise to more than 100 degrees Fahrenheit (37 degrees Celsius).

Heat bursts can be very dangerous. That's not just because of the heat. It's also because of the wind. A wind gust in a heat burst can be strong enough to knock down trees and rip roofs off buildings.

THE HEAT OF THE NIGHT

Heat bursts usually happen in the evening or during the night.

WHEN THE HEAT NEVER ENDS

A few hot days aren't so bad. But what if the heat lasts longer? Then, it's a heat wave!

Heat waves happen when warm air becomes trapped over an area. An area of high pressure pushes warm air down.

Some heat waves last just two or three days. But others last a lot longer! During a heat wave in the Great Plains in 1936, some places recorded more than 14 straight days of temperatures higher than 90 degrees Fahrenheit (32 degrees Celsius).

Temperatures in Fahrenheit July 5–18, 1936														
Locations	**7/5**	**7/6**	**7/7**	**7/8**	**7/9**	**7/10**	**7/11**	**7/12**	**7/13**	**7/14**	**7/15**	**7/16**	**7/17**	**7/18**
Decorah, IA	101°	106°	104°	101°	104°	103°	107°	101°	109°	111°	102°	103°	106°	100°
New Hampton, IA	106°	104°	102°	100°	100°	104°	104°	108°	110°	110°	106°	106°	104°	100°
Rochester, MN	92°	105°	102°	99°	101°	105°	104°	107°	107°	108°	100°	101°	102°	96°
Grand Meadow, MN	93°	104°	100°	97°	98°	103°	102°	105°	105°	106°	97°	100°	101°	96°
Mondovi, WI	90°	101°	100°	101°	195°	92°	106°	109°	109°	110°	101°	101°	100°	100°
Richland Center, WI	93°	100°	102°	100°	101°	103°	105°	108°	109°	110°	102°	97°	101°	94°
La Crosse, WI	94°	100°	104°	102°	102°	100°	104°	105°	106°	108°	95°	97°	101°	96°
Viroqua, WI	95°	100°	102°	102°	99°	98°	104°	106°	108°	108°	105°	96°	100°	102°

DATA FROM THE NATIONAL WEATHER SERVICE

Staying Safe in Heat and Cold

Heat waves can be very dangerous. Extreme heat can cause people to become **dehydrated**. Their body temperatures can rise too high. More than 5,000 people died in the 1936 heat wave.

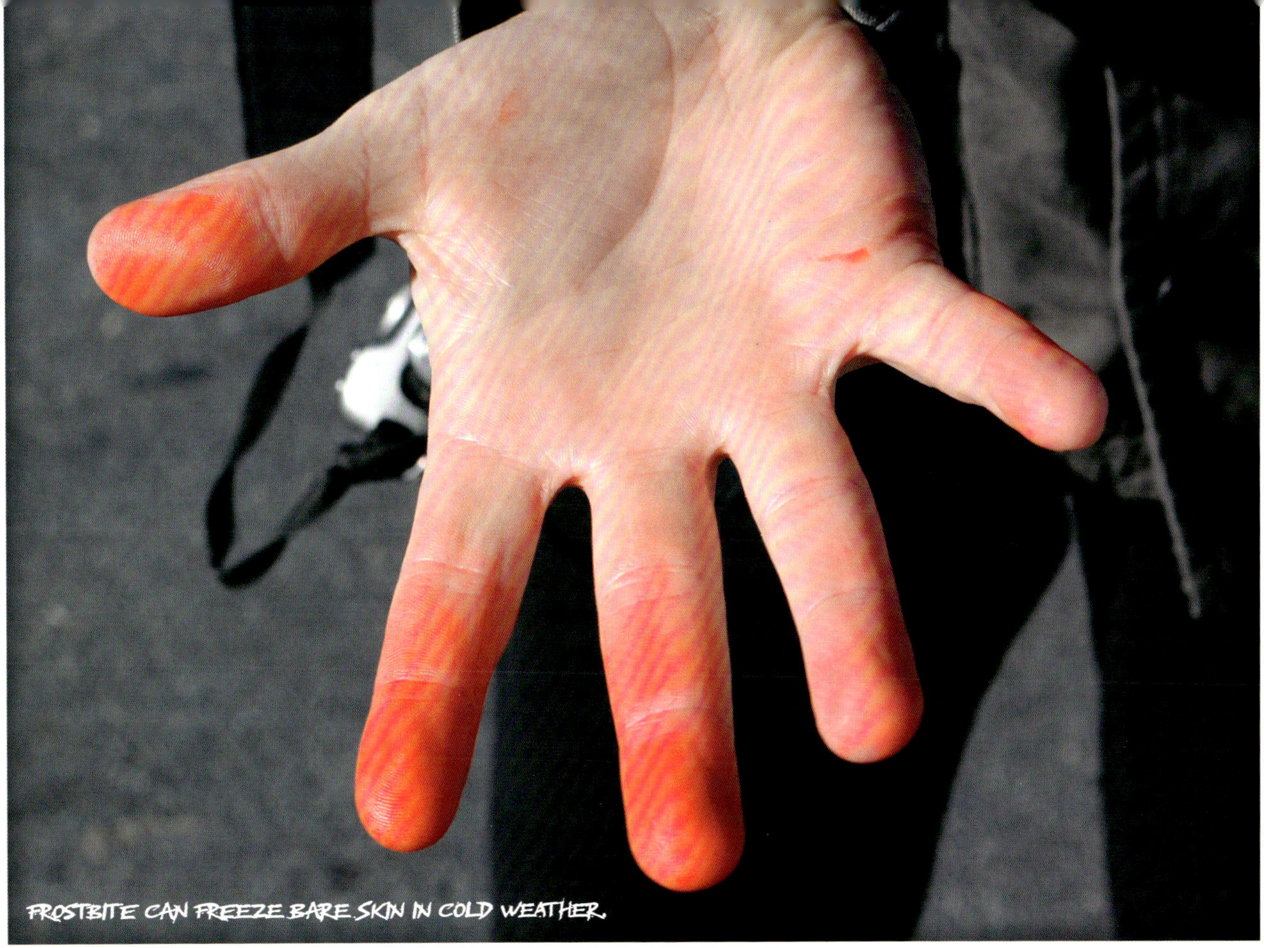

FROSTBITE CAN FREEZE BARE SKIN IN COLD WEATHER.

Extreme cold is dangerous too. People can freeze to death. They can lose fingers and toes to frostbite. It is important to be prepared so extreme weather does not hurt you! Listen to weather reports. Have supplies on hand. And check on your neighbors and friends!

WHAT AM I?

Can you guess which temperature extreme is shown in each photo? Look closely at these images and use the clues to help you figure it out. Then, check your answers below. How many did you get right?

1

Heat sits heavily on my dry land, but nights here are super-cold. What am I?

2

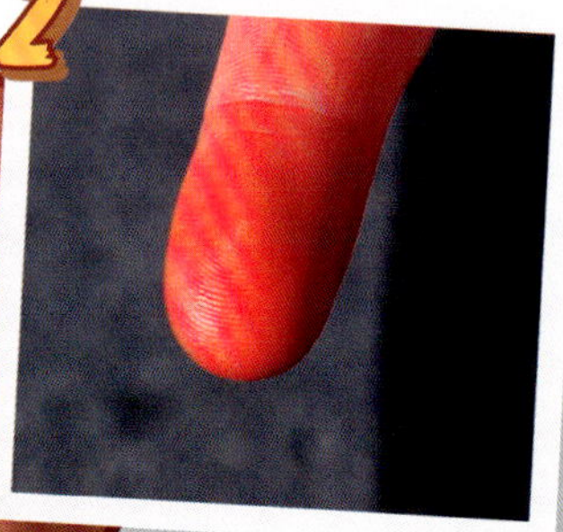

You'd better wear gloves when the temperature drops, or I might make your fingers sore and red. What am I?

3

A few days of my high temperatures and you'll be wishing for a change in the weather. What am I?

4

It's winter, but my warm air makes the snow melt and the temperature rise. What am I?

5

A change in the weather is on the way when I breeze through town. Better get your coats and hats! What am I?

1. hot desert; 2. frostbite ; 3. heat wave; 4. Chinook winds; 5. cold front

GLOSSARY

accurate (AK-yuh-rit): exactly right

dehydrated (dee-HYE-dray-tid): lacking enough water in your body

gradual (GRAJ-oo-uhl): happening slowly and steadily

instruments (IN-struh-muhnts): tools that scientists use to measure things

moisture (MOIS-chur): dampness

plateau (pla-TOH): an area of level ground that is higher than the surrounding area

precipitation (pri-sip-i-TAY-shuhn): the falling of water from the sky in the form of rain, sleet, hail, or snow

surface (SUR-fis): the outermost layer of something

FACT CHECK

1. During the day, temperatures in the desert can be very ________.
   a. hot b. cold c. comfortable
2. Chinook winds happen when warm air flows ________.
   a. over the ocean b. over a mountain c. along a river
3. Heat bursts often happen after a ________.
   a. blizzard b. cold front c. thunderstorm

Answers: 1. a, 2. b, 3. c

FURTHER READING

Abramson, Marcia. *Extreme Cold and Blizzards.* Bearport Publishing, 2024.
Crane, Cody. *Heat Waves.* Children's Press, 2025.
Tyler, Madeline. *Surviving an Ice Age.* Gareth Stevens Publishing, 2019.

ON THE INTERNET

Chinook Winds Facts for Kids
www.diy.org/article/chinook_winds
This article describes the causes and effects of Chinook winds and includes an interesting video.

What Is a Heat Wave?
www.nesdis.noaa.gov/about/k-12-education/understanding-our-planet/what-heat-wave
This article explains how heat waves form, the dangers they create, and how to stay safe.

Publisher's note to educators and parents: Our editors have carefully reviewed these websites to ensure that they are suitable for students. Many websites change frequently, however, and we cannot guarantee that a site's future contents will continue to meet our high standards of quality and educational value. Be advised that students should be closely supervised whenever they access the internet.

INDEX

ABOUT THE AUTHOR

Joanne Mattern is the author of many books for children on a variety of subjects, including science, history, and biography. She loves writing about and experiencing weird weather events! Joanne loves to learn about people, places, and events and bring historical figures to life for today's readers. She lives in New York State with her family.